TANYA

ALSO BY BRENDA SHAUGHNESSY

The Octopus Museum

So Much Synth

Our Andromeda

Human Dark with Sugar

Interior with Sudden Joy

TANYA

Poems

Brenda Shaughnessy

ALFRED A. KNOPF | NEW YORK | 2023

THIS IS A BORZOI BOOK
PUBLISHED BY ALFRED A. KNOPF

Published in the United States by Alfred A. Knopf,
a division of Penguin Random House LLC, New York,
and distributed in Canada by Penguin Random House Canada Limited, Toronto.

aaknopf.com

Knopf, Borzoi Books, and the colophon
are registered trademarks of Penguin Random House LLC.

Library of Congress Cataloging-in-Publication Data
Names: Shaughnessy, Brenda, 1970- author.
Title: Tanya : poems / Brenda Shaughnessy.
Description: First Edition. | New York : Alfred A. Knopf, 2023.
Identifiers: LCCN 2022023543 (print) | LCCN 2022023544 (ebook) | ISBN 9780593535936 (hardcover) |
ISBN 9781524712273 (trade paperback) | ISBN 9780593535943 (ebook)
Subjects: LCGFT: Poetry.
Classification: LCC PS3569.H353 T36 2023 (print) | LCC PS3569.H353 (ebook) | DDC 811/.54—dc23
LC record available at https://lccn.loc.gov/2022023543
LC ebook record available at https://lccn.loc.gov/2022023544

Jacket artwork: *Mirror,* 2022 by Clementine Keith-Roach / P·P·O·W, New York
Jacket design by Janet Hansen

Manufactured in the United States of America
First Edition

1st Printing

JUL 1 8 2023

For my mother, Mitsuko Higa, my first artist

The strange thing, on looking back, was the purity, the integrity, of her feeling for Sally. It was not like one's feeling for a man. It was completely disinterested, and besides, it had a quality which could only exist between women, between women just grown up.

—VIRGINIA WOOLF, *Mrs. Dalloway*

I paint flowers so they will not die.

—FRIDA KAHLO

CONTENTS

Saeculum

She was Woman of the Year that year. She got a plaque.

The next year they—those who chose Woman of the Year
each year—canceled the award for the foreseeable future.

It was decided that she, the last Woman of the Year, would become
the lifelong holder of the honor.

They engraved a dash on her plaque after the date she received her award,
to indicate its ongoingness unto death.

What did she do in all that time? With this one honor on her?
As a representative of the larger demographic body of herself?

She served until it finally became the sick joke it was always meant to be,
this defining achievement.

When she died, the plaque was amended—
after the dash they engraved the year of her death,

which was the last year the last Woman of the Year was Woman of the Year.

They—those who chose—had terms continually renewed amongst themselves,
but Woman of the Year died with her and her alone.

Since then, none of the Years had a Woman of it, though so many were worthy.

I

Moving Far Away

I hear they're trying to make borders in water now,
to declare it a place, impose a shape,
dissolve the solvent.

It's no solution to our probable problem:
I'll never see you again, I say on my cell. Said
to myself. We'll be well below alone now.

Can I be a good friend to you if I move so far away?
Haven't seen you in years but I like a rough edge—
island broken off a big bully,

I'll use up all my firewood on you.
Sorcery, what turned into me?
An iron foot, a leg of log. A wish for symmetry.

My fire handed down to me by cauldron witches
in their longish unauthorized youth—
broken crest rising,

rinsed of desire, full of pull and push no rush
to finish or to vanish. As if water didn't wave,
and bring tidings,

and answer me like an animal
jealous, crushed, washing herself.
I'll never forget you told me never to forget

but I did. Your voice a needle threaded
heading for my open wound,
already burned clean for a clean split.

Tell Our Mothers We Tell Ourselves the Story We Believe Is Ours

1.
The women created
the tunnels and the caves
for everyone.

Offering home or a place to hide,
space to be. To be held or hid
or helped to become old.

Blue stone, in nature,
is a trick of the eye,
a sky-trick, light playing air,

sky-diving into earth
to make you see it,
even if it's not there.

2.
"Now Dad's gone you can have fun."

"I could learn to have fun,
but I might never succeed,
and it seems like a waste of whatever
else I could have a chance to learn."

"Like puzzles? A new language?"

"Fun doesn't have to be learned
at all if you have it young enough.
But me—I'd have to work at it.
I don't know how to have fun."

She said that
as if someone else had said it to her.

3.
So I said: "Who told you
you 'don't know how to have fun'?"

"What?"

"You said 'One problem with me
is I don't know how to have fun,'

Did someone tell you that about yourself
or is that your own self-knowledge?"

"I think someone told me: you don't know
how to have fun

and I'd never thought about it before: fun.
My life was never fun.

I was a child and children have fun but
not me. Nobody looked after me
and I didn't even have the basics—
not enough was all I knew.

So when someone (your dad) told me
I didn't know 'how to have fun' of course
I believed him.

It was true. That's how I came to believe it,
I think, because of the truth of it. And also because
your dad said it was true."

But it can't be both.
But it can't be separated.

4.

CHAIN MAIL

If you do not copy this letter and mail it to six of your closest heart-friends (who adore you and think you'd have better judgment than to do this), you will experience radical misfortune that looks like fun/luck (not the sad event that nevertheless yields a golden river dawn). The following is just an example:

When the ceiling drops
the rain stops
beating down but
now you're beaten down

though it's the beat
that drops now
and we dance
in the rain
like sunbeams
made out of metal cloth,
tubes of blood,
and scared, sewn-up eyes.

5.

Then Dad left—
well . . . did he actually leave?

When he was with us he was intensely absent,
but when he physically left it seemed
he was effortlessly still there, still   "with us"?

There must be a difference,
and it can't be both
since one is fact (he left)
and one is fiction (he's here).

One is an act
and one is addiction.

6.

A story of how we travel	(because we want to or need to, rarely both.)
from painful lost-in-the-unknown	(are *you* my mother?)
and being left out	(in the rain, of the circle, to rot.)
to finding love	(which includes endlessly more than what's contained by the word of it but that container holds the map to find it.)
to finding love within	(the longest journey has the same repeating terrain—switchbacks, backtracks, circles— only to end up mere paces from the start.)
to making the world without reflect the world within	(is a magic. to imagine and to wonder fiercely, is *this* what we're meant to do in this life?)
and vice versa	(or is there something else? or is this only for artists?)
to heal both entry and exit wounds to repair the path between	(is *this* what we're meant to do in this life?)

but what if the path remains
broken, the wounds open

and the world wasn't reflected
either to or from itself

neither made nor made of

and we didn't find love within
and we didn't find love
and we weren't left out
so we didn't feel lost and alone

so we never traveled
but stayed here,
whether we wanted to
or needed to   (does that difference make all the difference?)

to try to find our true story.   (which may be nowhere, it's true.)

7.
Oh but what is the story, after all that?
it's not a straight line or a jagged one.

It's a spray cloud,
                    fast water hitting rock hard
                    and exploding,
                    then coming together to
                    settle back and go
                    the original direction
                    toward the sea.

The story is many spray clouds
                              and storm clouds
                                        wind storms, the breath of trees
                                        and other living things, off-gassing.
Clouds of natural gas.
Hot air. Cool breeze. Naturally. Unnaturally.

                                        But nothing's natural.
                                        And nothing's unnatural either.
                                        The original concept is off.
                                        Switched off.
Switch it on: that story is winding
both ways,
a short story that's taking forever.

8.
The story is a family
of inside and outside,

who begat grass underfoot
and green recycled siding,

who adopted wind energy
and gas guzzling. And invasive
species married in—

and winter vegetables
divorced out.

The heat and the cold grew up
unsupervised, basically, and can't
feel anything.

The flowers so automatically
attached themselves to your leg
as you try to run away

to find another shelter
you can afford
where, if time turns out
to be a good roommate,
you won't have to immediately
make plans to move again,

a thing that's called "to stay."

If we keep saying it,
the story might stay   (if it doesn't turn away from us)
and make its home in us,
will travel with us,   (unravel us)
will begin to understand
the family of itself
as it is delivered to us   (living in a grotto, moving to a cave,
as we are delivered to it.   through a tunnel a woman made.)

9.
Women cupped their hands
to make baskets
to catch babies
to carry and carry.

Women made the vessels
the tub the cup the jug
the mug, many things
with U in it, held by her
making and making.

Women made the jars
and pitchers to pour
themselves into,
to pour for you,
pouring and pouring
for everyone.

10.
The story is a rage/range
of hills and mountains
—anger dispersed over years
years ago—

that look and feel like a reclining
woman and nobody is offended
by this anymore.

Resting in middle age for energy
to make everything for everybody,
shortly, longingly.

She's the main character even though
she doesn't travel.

She is the traveled.

The Impossible Lesbian Love Object(s)
—after Meret Oppenheim's *Object*

1.
It's just an object, it's not me.

I'm more than an object, we are not having tea.

I am not one, not two. I am a feminist three.

I am Dada—not Mama, never will be.

When no one can use me, I am most free.

2.
I am not like other objects unaware
of themselves, those props subbing for desire:

the corner of the room thinks the room is one-cornered,
that cat sculpture staring as if with its eyes.

I, too, am a mammal stolen from my original sense of thirst.
Women know this disappearance from meaning.

Like all lesbian triptychs, I've stumbled.
Like all love objects, I am triangular, unstable.

I'm a lonely trio, a single setting, vexed
and passive, sexed and distracted.

A hot drink, a pot on the fire, the muscles
loosened, an inner stirring, a little spill,

the coat on the floor. The fur coat on the floor.
The curved fur floor atop another fur circle

to never catch a drop and a concave face
with convex back, swirling nothing.

None of it really happening.
I was once and always only ever an idea,

just a clever blip, a quip, a dare,
converted by coin and concept,

given body, shape, hair,
and an immortal uselessness

all art thinks it's born with,
that women can't get near.

3.
I'm beloved for being art's best worst idea.
Famous for being impossible,

that's why I'm obscene.
Not because everybody wants to fuck the cup,

not even the spoon can get it up.
Full frontal frottage, sapphic saucer,

a curving inside-outness, hairy leather hole.
Liquid's skill is soaking, then getting sucked.

Seed's luck is spilling, then being tilled.
It turns out we *are* having tea,

but it's all so heavy with life-cycles
that even when you go light, with art,

to get a little air, the room's still a bit dark.
And I'm repulsed, which attracts, in fact

the promise of warm fur is ancient,
will outlast the ritual fire and water

of tea for three, not two.
You see there's me, and you, and we.

Pelts melt into a new body, not old.
We're not thirsty—we're not cold.

4.
I'm not just an object,
my surfaces servicing,
but I'm no more than myself.

I end at my edges, finish my points,
even if I bend your senses,
when I am this soft.

The spoon is small,
the cup, generous,
the saucer extra absorbent—

past story, beyond end,
like a certain kind
of woman I have been with,
and been.

On *The Shaded Line* by Lauren Lovette
—for Georgina Pazcoguin

Who would believe she was not the pink
cloud, rainy and perfect

in the hot light circling
the dark center
of everyone's eyes?

Not me, if I hadn't seen.
To see what we believe: performance.
To be what we need: belief.

(I believe I needed to see her
to know what I needed to see.)

And there she was:
black shoes, white shirt,
no skirt, no friends.

No flood of tulle to pull
her down to drown with the other birds

who can't fly till thrown into air.
She throws, and the music rose,
with scream,

to lift her lifting.
It's not a gift. It cost everything.
In case you thought it was easy.

A woman's body is born to be,
born for her to be in.

It should be a given. It's not
born to wear, to wear out,
worn out, warned, contorted.

A dress is not address, where you live.
A dress is addressed to you, yes,
assigned to you, but not a sign you're you.

So why should the dancer's body
tell only one side of one story?

Why not change my mind like a dress—
like the wind changes trees.

A woman is not a tree
but she can lift the wind
with her limbs.

A dancer wise and rising
with the breath that is music
riding the air—what does she wear?

Why must it matter? Does it fly her?
Does it let her move
like animals in their skins?

Where has she been?
Lifting women and leaving shoes

as she crosses the strange wide water
between flower and force
flow of blood and air,

smudge and rise and curve and bow
and flex and push and hide and widen

and open

and going.

What a dancer might do
if her feet were as free as hands
waving goodbye, waving come in.

Who Sings Whose Songs?
—after Torkwase Dyson's *Sing*

Who will decide once and for all: half-empty or half-full?

Will it be left to the artist—(is it right for an artist? Is it the right of an artist?)
    to weigh and lay
to rest the question of half, of division, of border, of definition, of edge?

Is that the artist's realm?

That power, that naming force: semi is a half-curl, hemi is a cup, demi a
    reduction.
But half of an infinite form is more than can ever be drained drunk diminished
    or determined.

Must we trust the artist to give us perspective, to give us proper proportions?
Ask an artist at the dinner party and put everybody on edge.

It doesn't go over well. Doesn't go down easy.
Leave the table to its surface dimensions, service, salt.

Turn your face, an eclipse in cups, a rim aswim in a stemless wineglass.
I'm glass. See through me.

Drink the moon, your reflection, your bottomless river.
A swarm aswirl as well.

Where else does gravity lead if not to the grave?
Why does water bead up on not wet what can't be bathed?

Who can tell me if this is:

                An architect's drawing of whiskey on spherical ice.

                A cross section of a skipped stone mid-skip?

                A dream of taking a bath.

Whale approach.

You, Just Barely Touching My Arm.

Noted: Tiny triangle of intensity in the corner is actually
                                        the aperture, and we, the observer,
                                        will be in this picture.

Noted: Tiny corner triangle pointing out the way (uppish)
                                        to large circle half-submerged.

                                 Too many syllables, too many beats for this thing to
                                        sing from its Cubist face.

                                 With eye that closes from the bottom.

How are you holding up?

It makes me feel free, to look at this.

Questions of construct, boundaries, gradations, levels, areas, shapes, tones,
      dimensions . . .

are all worked out for me, who looks freely at the artist's work.

Who decides what displaces who?
When you came in the cup was full
so who sloshed out when you came in
and when did you decide to come
and push who down? How are you holding up?

Precise angles exist already everywhere in this wet air,
each new cup and shelf and ridge/edge/wedge/selvage
is salvaged
from an eternal original
mined
for usable dimensions.

Lines and curves recognize each other, like long lost.

Populations displace people—once places held space
for people, now only for a populace who can afford popular places—

replacing people with populace & allowing populations
to use places to replace people
& make places impossible to afford
so the people can't possibly return, long lost.

Fingerprints on a glass look inked in blood,

the iron rusting on its own home fluid:

nothing can be kept out for good.

Glass looks slick but it's made of:

many small staggered fissures, each little dagger cuts its bit of air

bit your tip like a mosquito, leaving a tiny blue pool under the skin.

How rare is something just entirely itself.
Not even water is.

How rare is something just entirely itself.
Not even water is.

A fingerprint is unique, yes, but now it's used for ID and not its ridges & whorls,
    for which
there is no standard of beauty.

Everything's used
is different than
everything is of use.

Who makes the call—what is in/what is out—whoever has the most objective sight
    line?

The artist's eye sees past vision, past even the notion of vision or the glimmer of
    the notion—
but gives voice to motion.

Who is on edge, in the drink, sink or swim, waving, draining, drowning, drawing,
    setting,
settling, sunk?

Who is singing, who sung?

On *Loss of Feathers* by Ursula von Rydingsvard

The hand had a soft surface with firm, padded hills on one side
and hard longish seawalls on the other. Opening this hand meant
pouring out all the moves that made so many pictures and paintings
—those portraits and portals—and looking at the spout, the route.

Where, on its way, did an idea become a physical object? At what point in the
    creative process?
When thought became action, was it in the first moment of action that thought
    gained a materiality
of sorts, a seedliness?

Or does an idea retain the essence of thinker-spirit as long as it's being thought,
    thought through,
and throughout the making process, and when the making is finally over, only
    THEN does the idea,
now something more than just the idea, dump the product itself plus the making
    process,
into the product itself. The made thing then becoming itself the moment it's
    finished.

No that can't be right. It has to be the first, right?
Thing becomes thing as soon as it begins to become itself.

No government criminalizes abandoned art projects, even though the promise,
the very spark of independent life, might be there.

The artist's hand is always open, even if it's holding something. Especially so.

It has to be. The artist's hand guides the horizon of seeing to the very
edge, overlapping, even layering the way you must to cover something
completely. Feathers cover tightly to keep the line of liquid out, wicking
it away.

Birds can't get their skin wet or something? It's a tight weave—waterproof like skin
    is,
not like hair, which is about warmth.

Warm skin, cold feathers. Cold weather, warm clothes. New form, old function.

Decades ago, the much older woman, an artist, took my arm and said:
"Look at this strong little arm" and marveled, her hand stroking me fingertip to
    elbow.
I was embarrassed. I thought she was envying my young body.

Many years later, now that I envy my own young body, I realize she wasn't coveting
    mine
but finally claiming her own.

We held hands, looked at each other's. Turned them over and around. Feathery age
    spots,
neater freckles, blue ridges and knuckle dimples, wrist wrinkles that go across.
Blood traversing its own known way and never crossing another's.

She said you couldn't be an artist and a mother back then. It was impossible, then
    suddenly unsure,
she said, well, impossible for her. Being a mother, she never wanted to. Lucky she
    didn't have to.
Her arms were for art. Her hands, her fingers in mine, which would make art deep
    into a future
that was done being hers. That had transferred to me.

The idea becomes art, alive, the moment of conception. The eventual object may
    only be a pinprick
at that moment, and it may never develop. Or it might.

The process of making—dissolving idea into body, body into thing, where thing
    emerges, made.

That one feather, lost, to the bird, on its many-minded journey, is never missed.

Another feather finds its place. But the art was the only one of its kind. And I
    continue on
into a future which won't be mine the way her hand in mine was mine.

On *Romeu, "My Deer"* by Berlinde De Bruyckere

One of a years-long, multi-media, genre-crossing series, aren't we all?

This one, two-dimensional, a study, a page, barely an object, barely more than
    speech in the air,
a blur, script on paper, existing fragile low and shallow with its corners, yet
    grasping
for the space I occupy.

The other "Romeu My Deers" stick out of the wall, grabbing into the room from
    the other side
of the Deer-mirror, death-lamped.

The others have their own bodies to inhabit. Don't they all?
Yet they search mine out. Yours too. His. Others are hungry, others need territory
    too.

This page-bound body is tampered-with with hands, hands withdrawn, body left
    half-turned,
tuned-in, half-stood, misunderstood hardwood, with no hands, good
    regenerative genitals
as if to say:

We meet again.
We: meat, again?

And again, we come. We return.
Buttressing an arch through which we are welcomed.
We.
By "we" I mean "me."
In this way the self lives forever.

Me at work
Meatwork.
A done deal.   Cooked.

Flesh meat hard with flexion, opening to the murderous air, inside the body
air must not flood itself,
or death,
again, seated for every meal.

Torso pointing up as if Prometheus awaiting carrion birds to begin uploading him,
aching to be hung from the sky.

There's so little freedom in the circulatory system, there is no flying, only the
    hunger
to offer oneself up to whatever is hungry. To whatever smells death for its living.

Amazing angles, peaceful pieces, gestural suggested musculature as speculative
    architecture:
                a portrait of a torso pinned in place by limbs.

The body is a pot brimming over a fire—foot and knee on fire, head in the air,
arched back offering
                penile wood
                vaginal water
                bending back body—this viscous process.

Prominent, frontal, in deepest hue, is penis, it's true the dark pink taint splits in
    two,
splotched vulvar
with vagina viewed wholly as X-ray.

I am surprised by the body restarting itself, the mind relieved of the total burden
and signaling,
through the body, that audible relief.

Relief also visible in the body's planes and hills, geography as much as any
    occupied territory.

And in the background, presupposed but unseen, your hand moving swiftly to
     strike me,
scoop me affectionately, show me where to go, or supposing, superimposing,
     shaking,
waving goodbye.

But I keep looking at you, so close to opening.

For the Matter to Mean and the Meaning Matter
—for Toba Khedoori

It isn't itself, ever. If it was made—and it always was made—then it is of other.

But other is always itself, ever changing, like clockwork.
Its ideas of what it is: as many as there are stars.

But stars don't grasp at ness-ness as it does. As we do.

•

To find the ness-ness is the process of making something into itself.
It's an inexact art, so we use metaphors.
We say this other thing is in fact this thing.

That's a kind of opposite approach, but there are no opposites.
There are only dimensions, relations, recurrence, series.
We might say life is like another life.

A fire is what it burns to make itself fire.
A door becomes something else when opened.
Both many miles and zero miles walked back and forth across the same halls.

You walked but went nowhere. Same on roads. A road leading nowhere,
or leading everywhere? A road takes less time to travel if you go fast
but if there is no destination it takes no time.

Time disappears sans endpoint. From any viewpoint
there is key information out of sight. Any way is far.
Even a dead end ends in a place, and even that isn't an end.

There is still road and traveler. Distance covered is a matter
of matter and maybe a pinch of a dream
of time if you can fall asleep long enough to believe it.

•

"It's all uphill from here" means tough going.
"It's all downhill from here" means deterioration.
And when the road is level—and it is never level—there is still the question:

Are you going away or toward? Neither and both, in any instant.
No matter how far we go we cover such little ground.
Space surrounds, enclosing us like an open-wire fence.

•

You think you are waiting for the image to resolve, for the light to change, for the metaphor to force the meta, for the representation to present itself again, for the line to move, for the room to fill, for the matter to mean and the meaning matter, for the time to pass (pass as what? As reality? As space?). Waiting to fill out the form, waiting for the form to function. To turn up, to turn the corner, to turn the page.

But you are not waiting. You are turning, your solutions resolutions. You are burning and you are empty and you are time passing through you like a broken window. You are misunderstood fire in your indeterminate house. You are road, light, line, door, rooms, endlessly changing and in that changeability ever the same.

You are a room in a building and you are building the building. You are each empty chair in all the rows of empty chairs and the ones that didn't make it into the room. You're up in smoke. You don't go anywhere. You are railings that never touch, roomless windows. You are what's between inside and outside, including the separating membrane. Even though all this is your entirety, you can't imagine how little you contribute to all this, for there are endless amounts of all this, and the smallest portion constitutes all of you.

Yes, it is endless, but that's just one way of looking at it, as endlessness is an estimate, we've never been able to prove it, and it's gone in a blink.

You open the door—it disappears. You disappear into ever more of it.

•

These half-built houses: destroyed or mid-construction? No matter the answer, no one lives there. Still we look for ourselves in these ruins or in that future, half-believing some half-finished half-razed self has only been half-projected onto it.

A tree knows that what is beyond itself is also itself. Knows it's constituted by soil, sun, air, water, fire, paper, pulp, plank, half-built house/destroyed house, door, leaf, ash, seed, and breath. Our breath.

One person, that tangle of matter and energy, that bag of broken clocks dreaming of ness-ness, can never be only that one person nor the entirety of that person, but they can be more.

We know there's something beyond our shadow triangulating to trick us into
        thinking
we are complete, formed, solid. We know there's something beyond it
even if all we know is that we know.

•

Sometimes you're a tangle, like a memory or wood branches in the snow, and this disordered state will soon change. Not toward order but away from this particular disordered state. Soon you'll be a door, one of many in many rows of doors leading inward as much as they lead out. A mere means. An idea of entry and exit.

The door, once we're through it, disappears and the road remains as an idea of
        travel,
travel's shadow. We block the light in order to step through the door and onto the
        road.

Where there is shadow, there is light, a kind of fire. Part star, part ash. Fire throws shadows but doesn't have one of its own. We remember the house we left is an idea of not-traveling.
if memory is shadow, time is fire.

•

Fire looks like life; a representation looks like fire. But fire isn't life.
It is not spirit, not passion, though there are shared qualities.
Fire is a contained energy, a chemistry, a speck of nature.

Fire has a self-parasitic golden rule: what it does
—consume, warm, lick, suffocate, burn, melt, destroy—
is done to itself as well.

We like to control a piece of fire and look at it. We know we mustn't let it find
full expression, its full potential. It must be kept smaller than it is.
We like to overpower fire's power.

Sometimes we decorate the fireplace with pictures so when there is no fire to look
   at
we can look at something else we like to look at.
A picture of a fire is fire twice overpowered, and perhaps we enjoy that even more,

believing there is less to fear.
But even a picture of a fire in a box on a page is flammable.
The heat is metaphoric, and thus can't be doused.

A picture of a fire comforts: it isn't alive. The live fire in the fireplace is cozy
and under control. And we the living, burning with life?
Cold soon, too, just ash.

A fire is what it burns, until burned.
A road does not travel: one travels it.
A road cannot take you anywhere. You must take it.

The Artist Jessica Rankin

loves poetry.
I love artists who love poetry
(Dorothea Tanning was another)
because artists know what they
create sounds well beyond the edge
of the visual realm. They know
poetry uses vision from a corner
of the palette, a couple blobs
of paint dipped into for highlights
and shadow. Artists love edging
and spilling over into fresh media,
mesh nets spread to catch them.

Who will tell the capacious, frank,
and po-sexual artist Jessica Rankin
that poetry thinks music contains
the attributes the artist attributes
to poetry? That poetry leans hard
on music so constantly that music
doesn't even notice the parasitic
pressure and sponge anymore.
Music's got better things to do
and is not really in a hurry the way
poetry and art sorta seem to be.

Maybe the dancer Georgina will be
asked to perform yet another task
for another's art. Asked to give her
body's limited editions of breath
and blood, her lifetime's supply.
How relentless to embody another's
creation! How necessary, this vexed
vesseling, voice-over-like: not even
music stands on its own without
instruments, and instruments
need players, players need bodies,

bodies need choreography to move
the music out of its resting place,
unsettle the score.

The score, yes, Paola wrote more
than the staff can handle, so lush
on the page the old idea of an opera
on a plain four-corner stage grows mold.
She knows who broke the music—
those who chose to kill it young rather
than have to learn to hear anew.
I'm thinking the choreographer
Lauren—who is young, who grew up
in my hometown decades after I left—
might have something to say about
the institutions in which all our art's
contained, meted out, cut, maimed.

I'll get blowback for saying that.
People who insist on controlling art
will say this isn't art: good. Ignore it.
Too late. I'm interrupted now, here
—no, you're asking—in the middle
of a poem, why I'm dropping names?
I'll namecheck if I please but, please,
I'll not drop these names. I pick them,
from the artistree to graft onto poetree.
It is, you know, a "high art" and I am
a poet, classically fancy. Just ask
Jessica. Poetry's still up there,
living light in a high-rise, editing
the edifice's artifice. Sky-struck.

This poem is only a net (fish-, ether-)
for the artists gathered here in the way
of poets: cornered in a spiraling room
in case they, in the way of poets,
trip the edge and need a soft place

to land. Here: pulsing cloud pillows
with jackknife for the dancer, silk
hagiography for the choreographer,
true wave via childhood for Paola,
dreamy azure drops and lucent streaks
of aubergine (Dorothea's favorite
word) for the artist Jessica Rankin,
who loves poetry.

She Stands

—for Jennie C. Jones

Jennie I wrote a poem for you
in my first book but I'm not proud.
It was hard to know it was you, did you
see it was so crowded in that open book
of my closed eyes which should have seen
you through more disappointing lovers
and your mother's death and stayed open
to keep watch to make sure you made it
home, to your lifelong art, safely.

Sometimes in my life and home far
from you I think about how it felt between
us—innocent magnetic sparks, a love swirl
that had to be impossible, right? Wasn't it?
It couldn't really feel like that, no?
If it wasn't impossible and really felt
like that then why do I live without you
like this, without even talking?

Jennie I should have looked for you!
I shouldn't have let it get weird between us!
Did I disappear and you flew or did I fly
and you grew a new way and I didn't see
or stay? Why don't I remember if it was
only me who was afraid or you too?

Now all this time has passed and I look
at your art instead of your face and I'm
lost on your map and clock—I'm missing
your aging every day and I'd so wanted to
know which hair turned silver and when.
And you mine. How'd I lose all this time?

I hope you know I loved you then
and still do, I never turned the page

from the poem I wrote for you. Here
it is in a different frame and hue—I try to keep
it simple but it never was, I never could,
never outgrew the name you gave me,
which nobody knows or remembers but we.
I swear I'll give you this before you turn fifty-three.

The Poets Are Dying

It seems impossible
they seemed immortal.

Where are they going
if not to their next poems?

Poems that, like lives, make do
and make that doing do more—

holding a jolt like a newborn,
a volta turning toward a god-load

of grief dumped from some heaven
where words rain down

and the poet is soaked. Cold
to the bone, we've become. Thick-

headed, death-bedded, heartsick.
Poets. Flowers picked, candles wicked,

forgiving everyone they tricked.

Afterlife

I remember lying there
Trying to make a new memory

By folding aside existing ones
Like tablecloths

Protecting the presumed surface
Of a hole eaten through
My lost face.

Urv Predicts the Pres(id)ent

—for Urvashi Vaid (October 8, 1958–May 14, 2022)

She saw the present
so clearly—

she told Barack Obama:
*you aren't paying enough attention
to the right wing.*

And he answered, so lightly: *oh I'm not paying enough attention to the right wing?*

—that she knew we'd never get past it.

What Have I Done?

I was weak, or strong, depending—not interested in judging it now.

I let myself feel what I felt for a person, opened up my need
like a sentence I'd ever serve—a line never-ending, full of song
the air around me kept, cupped, to my always ear.

Now I must prepare for a soundlessness
to be my true time—I'll lose you to something,

if not to this.

I was foolish, headlong, afraid of having nothing—what's wrong with nothing?

I set myself to making you—a new person, if you died I'd die
just that simple. Aren't we simple? You live I live.
You my baby, my hurt perfect one I live in fear for.

Why did I make you, destroyer?
Honey on the wound but the wound is already clean,

having cut you from me, me from you.

I was insolent, stubborn, had to have my way—where was I going?

In debt, myself, to the accident of love I was born into,
was a criminal of. I owed back my air, my word,
every dog and child and poem and lover.

Who do I submit it all to? Who takes them all—everyone
I love—away, and where but where is away?

I believed. I held on. I thought that meant

I could have them.

II

Coursework

—for Helene Moglen

1.

For bodies, for the feelings flowing
              between bodies, is it time or space
                  that is most like mind?
                      Time to be together—together time tethers us
                         to longer longing.

The space between coasts,
              lived through like cats
                in heat, a TV set on staying on.
                      Farewell to the future's favorite fruit
                      all turned to juice.

We were fine right
           where we were when
              I was run from home
                  free from fire I forgot
                      you lit deep and holy-strong.

I was feral in the forest.
             Left behind a carbon of us
                to walk through woods on foot, in print
                      to read later.

2.

Thirty years ago you taught me that books can become

the beginning of a self—combine with a life in progress

to make a parallel story lived alongside, inside books.

That reading could mix with experience, making life

after life after life inside a solid simultaneous self.

You would lead me to that place books always promised:

where anything could happen but it was a matter of context—

place and time and body and politics—the analysis of which

was a mix of judgment and soul, of egos and logos and trust

that everything that happened in books happened inside us.

Once we got it straight that what should happen in books

echoed and sang with what we wanted to happen in life:

   a fair shot for women and girls

   a path from past racism to futureless racism

   and how to see the forest for the trees

   we walked through on our way to class,

   late, but not too late.

   Only ten minutes past thirty years later.

   Maybe too late for the trees

   now pages for the voice, the story with momentum

   older than fundament

   and twice alive, these lives of the women we

   were and the way our art and books stacked up

   to look like freedom of thought, and was it not?

3.
Helene had a map of the forest
in which were hidden an unknown number of paths
leading to the place where the key to the self was hidden,

the key to the doors of the self which might or might not
be hidden or might not exist, might not be the right doors
to what might not be the right self,

or the right path, or the map itself was hidden, safely inside
the self itself. Years to find it, decades defined it, a journey
folded up and saved and carried, carefully underlined.

4.
Didn't everything become, once you said it out loud?

A student in our class once said, out loud:
"I left the theater after a movie and caught a glimpse of someone in the mirror I
    didn't recognize as myself."

And, Helene, you said in reply: "yes, you look at a sunset and find that you are
    weeping."

It was a suddenly recurring moment we were all stunned to recognize

that it was only at this moment we recognized all the ways we did not recognize
    ourselves

until that moment, when we knew we knew we saw ourselves

and knew we knew we were each other.

And hidden in this clarity was our new knowledge that emotions were sensory,

that is: emotions had a way in and out of the body through senses,

and that reading cracked our glass covering and fit the tip

to our senses through which our bodies learned to read.

That my inner feelings and thoughts could be touched, contacted, radioed, by the
    outside world

and that I could transmit my own inner reality to the outside world if I made a
    material, sensory object to carry them out—

writing, art, music—those were the ways, the work, the course of the vessels.

I had to know how that work worked
how that way was made
so I could learn to make it myself.

And reading with Helene was how I would begin
or continue to go deeper, serious, way out of my depth.

I became a writer by becoming a reader—
this fact lifted confusion clear out of the page.

5.
We were in a graduate literature seminar

                    I didn't belong in.

Wendy talked you into admitting me

                    against your better judgment.

You knew I wasn't ready

                    I never did get ready

but I was pinkish, ambitious

                    and you could see how much I wanted

to become a serious reader worth the work.

That it was already a miracle I had found a way

                    to the desire to possess a serious mind

of my own. That I could go deep into reading

                    and find the world there, the mirror-page

refracted through my own weak light.

6.
I'm speaking of the past,
and of what passed, back then, as past:

We thought you had to already know something
before you could begin to learn it—

like having to speak a new language so the swim coach knows you're fast.

So many things like that, so many olympics before you ever opened your mouth.

Pre-learning. But pre-learning was all desire—whatever you wanted.
    Polymorphous.

Books prepared you for other books.

I told Helene I only wanted to read books by women—
that should tell you where I was at back then.

And Helene disapproved, and pushed Henry James on me, a small one,

Turn of the Screw, and I opened my mind not only to psychological torment

as metaphor for attachment & projection

but that book kept me from re-framing the world in the name of only-ever
    feminism,
—to resist the lure of totalizing every book just to feel power over it.

7.
Donna you taught me books were seven-dimensional: text, supporting text, length, width, time, energy, belief.

Bettina you taught me that to become a woman I would need to seriously grow up, to see ordinary days as heart-stopping continual historical facts.

Wendy you taught me personhood was powerful and not a given—it had to be continually re-written in ever stronger language, deeper ink.

Helene you made books live inside me, like parasites or worms dangerously close to my heart, ever after a book-heart, deceiving digesting discovered continually.

Villette is Charlotte's best book, *Beloved* is America's most necessary and visionary
    book,
Mrs. Dalloway showed the gendered split between two worlds—I wrote a poem
called "Postfeminism," which begins:

"There are two kinds of people, soldiers and women, as Virginia Woolf said. Both
    for decoration only."

To whom was I writing if not you, my teachers, to show you that your teaching took, that what you taught caught, released back into the current as writing, as poetry, living talk.

8.
It wasn't easy to get to Helene's 10 a.m. class on Tuesdays and Thursdays.

The bus station was always so crowded with people going up to campus, you
    couldn't squeeze onto the first or second bus, had to wait for a third.

If you tried to catch a bus further along the route, they'd all pass you without stopping, loaded.

I finally got on a bus and tried to use the ride to finish the reading for class—I was behind, as usual. I lingered over *Mrs. Dalloway* so long I often forgot where I was.

I didn't have a seat, jostled between the patchouli and hummus bodies.

Almost crushed, I found the passage in Woolf that opened my life and changed my cells and flung my funny underused little heart straight into love's and literature's fire. Literature was love and love was lit.

"Then came the most exquisite moment of her whole life passing a stone urn with flowers in it. Sally stopped; picked a flower; kissed her on the lips. The whole world might have turned upside down! The others disappeared; there she was alone with Sally. And she felt that she had been given a present, wrapped up, and told just to keep it, not to look at it—a diamond, something infinitely precious, wrapped up, which, as they walked (up and down, up and down), she uncovered, or the radiance burned through, the revelation, the religious feeling!"

How did Woolf know when she wrote that that I was in love too? With *that*!

Everything in my life made a certain new sense, after that moment in which it was clear that Clarissa loved Sally Seton.

Years later, in New York, I would love a woman named Sally for that reason alone.

That should tell you where I was at back then.

It was the most romantic thing I'd ever read.

I loved it down to the syntax, to the parataxis.

I studied it obsessively like you would a lover's pinky's second knuckle. Those semi-colons.

It was not for some role, it was not for show
not for experience or learning to suppress your wants.
It was NOT what someone else wanted from me it was what I wanted
and that was so new it was life-altering, hallucinogenic.

The drugless derangement, book love, this love. All I wanted was for it to
    continue.

Woolf killed herself eventually—is that what love did?

But there was Helene, alive, showing us too what love did, how it helps us live.
And live I did for love; I did I lived for lit and for love.

It was Sally not Clarissa I longed to be—when I wasn't afraid.

Sally—who let the rain ruin borrowed books.

Woolf spoke through Helene when Helene spoke of Woolf,

and worked the ontological question—who was Clarissa? Who was Septimus?

Who were we as bodies and minds?

How can we sleep at night?

Who are we as a species

that we would lose so much to hate and fear and despair

and who are we as people to love each other the way we still do?
The way we still yearn to.

9.
I still have the books we read for your classes.

After leaving California I kept your books close,
always on my best shelves, at eye-level,

through thirteen moves in twenty New York years.
I think of them as your books.
Their spines encoded mine.

The Bonds of Love, for example,

taught me about transference

which I was always having, heavily.

You showed me how I could counter it, in my own teaching future,

by countering mine, then.

Nobody ever taught future teachers how to do that—

how to handle the boundary-seeking, desperate, love

so achy and misdirected, of a student for a teacher?

Of course it's erotic love. Reading is erotic, sharing language,

bodies and minds across time and space.

Helene alone tended the boundary as she would a border of flowers

others trampled or picked.

10.
I must have fallen in love in that classroom fifteen times. With classmates, with
the teacher, with the authors, their characters, their characters' metaphors.

What else is a meta for?

What better way to learn than through love?

With a woman you could trust to keep love moving around the room like music,

like we were the music, a chorus of private readers rising on waves of words and
 voice

and following the lines and rolling in the meaning and noting all the beauty

and falling in love all before turning the page again and again.

And next week, again. And again on Thursday.

Literature snapped into place the way flowers know how to attract.

A story was a lived theory, a template, a windbreak,

an immortal lived theory, as the story continues, all echo and breath.

This chain of life is made of letters the writer writes to the reader.

Coursework is the letter written back to the writer.

Then the writer writes again, another book, a response it seems
to our class discussion—we read deeper into it.

The author is dead but we imagine she's exchanging letters with us, the readers of
the future,

reading ahead, catching up.

In this way the writing lives on.

The author was you, Helene. You wrote so much of me. Pre-wrote what came to be.

I'm writing back to you, although you can't hear me in sense and self,

it's still a back and forth in time and space, still a take and give.

I'm writing back to you for whom to read was to live.

III

Tanya

I.

What are we if we stop
    knowing each other?
      As if I never knew you,
         never loved
           the shoulders and spine and eyes
             that turned you back

to me over and over, never again to
    not get enough before it's over—
       is it already over?
         The wind slams the door shut
           on our time together
             is just a draft

not a polished work of art,
    maybe future-finished, maybe
      future-known, worth saving
        in some box way back. A scrap blown
          away or burned up somehow
            wound up wind.

There is no future
    why wait?
      There is no why
        why ask?
          Why is there a concept of future
            to ask after

to wait for an answer from?
            Asking, in itself, is hope
                  the way the disappearing road is both
                        a way and a question: where you're going will you
                              take me will you take me with you
                                      if you go?

Will you go the way going goes
              or will you go the way
                    the way goes?
                              Taking not even yourself
                                  just disappearing right
                                      into where you left.

Everyone's not-you to me
                but you are "you" to the others
                    whose "yous" haven't left them.
                              They think you won't leave them.
                                I know you too well to ask:
                                    whose "you" are you?

You said—we all said—
              each of us was a "you" to each of us:
                  cherished, hand on knee, wet face.
                            I know you now and forever
                              my blood and water,
                                    my sealed bag.

Who needs a future if you'll go away
              into it, leaving me here
                with only the you of now,
                    so soon past,
                        our future split pants
                        to laugh at, then throw out.

So many you didn't reconnect with
                    get in touch with
                              reach out
                                        to well neither did you
                                                  old neighbor, once-love, bad friend
                                                                      I got tired of.

Worth loving once, why not now?
                    Unloved, might as well be dead—
                              it's why we write, right?
                                        To live twice, two chances to be loved.
                                                  Dead anyway. And the love goes
                                                            where? Where the love was,

        is where it lives, now learning to live alone.
                    Unloved love learning to live alone—
                              maybe I could do it:
                                        let life be books, supplies,
                                                  silently using ingredients,
                                                            floral ups and downs. Decor.

Every day a "well I'm alive" day.
                    Or grab it all back?
                              You are not dead my love has a home.
                                        I made our time last
                                                  like last time,
                                                            how I made it last all night

and into the morning, this "it"
                    being our night and morning. Ours, ours.
                              Hours and hours. We don't count
                                        them. They are countless we don't count
                                                  we are counted on. I draw letters
                                                            on your back, spelling out spells

which are unsung on maps.
        The words naming the ways
                have meaning to speak of
                    and they line
                          every page I write on your back,
                              the map endless this way.

II.

"You"—my friend I made and lost, I did not write
                you, will never know the end of you
                   that's not how I write anyway,
                        knowingly. I swear your
                            hand is little but you
                                carry me. I'm liquid-heavy.

But "you" are also me, before, during, later, over
                 the foil, the lover, the ham & cheese
                     who will not eat herself.
                        Veganly, you undo yourself
                            in hopes that after a time
                            you can sneak back in.

I don't care if this is general,
              pointless, unaware what it is
                 only you will read it and you know
                      it's all true. No going back to fix us.
                          we evaporated & are air like
                              everyone else's.

I've tried so hard to trick myself
              into realness, to escape
                the artificial ingredients
                     cooked into me. So dissembling &
                     uncremating & separating & reversing
                          the processes is how I—

Oh that can't be right—what a fool.
              I mistook a wish for a tool.
                    Hammered my own crate shut
                      shipped off to stranger water
                          than I imagined. That was no trick
                            that was just me,

wanting to believe a realness
                I could believe in existed
                        somewhere I didn't make or visit
                                —that I could land home somewhere,
                                        call someone on a landline,
                                              call these lines mine.

Didn't I find myself
                unbearable, mostly? And you annoyed me
                        as much as amazed me. Always
                                interrupting sorry but but but likely
                                      you were right to cut me
                                              off every time I began?

I had written something ugly here—
                something mean I can't walk back
                        but now you want to know
                              what I erased. I can tell you
                                  it was true, and only about myself.
                                      There, now we're less interested,

no? Yes. Time can't erase it but I can,
                still. It will have to do. The ones I loved
                    who died—why do I say I "loved" why "died"
                            why not "The ones I love who die"
                                since that's what I'm presenting here:
                                  I love them, they still die. I am there

in that time
                when I love them,
                    I am with them
                        because I speak of it now.
                              If their death is past,
                                  so should my love for them be

but I hold their death inside
         my living love.
              If this death is past tense, rigor'd,
                    my love isn't.
                       Is a hot, wet, stinging hole
                          I came to fill with you, instead.

Wasted time piles up like plastic watches
         behind the internet
         full of phish
                how can I make jokes
                   at a time like this, having wasted
                       what little I had

on a thought I never finished, a cake
         still goo inside, though it is already decorated
            to look like a graveyard in the sun
               blinking hard
                and seeing nothing
                  but nobody singing behind trees.

III.

An old spark may stay true, if you want.
A new one the same.
How can I write to you?
Shouldn't every utterance be worthwhile?
Mustn't it be, to get past the censors?
Aren't the censors us, each of us

daring the other to prove it?
If I think it through, the idea's inert—
if I don't, it's half-baked.
What is thinking's chemistry?
"Say more things" said the little girl
I had dazzled by saying

a few weird words
but I suddenly had no more.
Who waits for their thoughts
to develop like film
or fever? A thought's moment isn't made
of time, though measured in time.

Thought is made of mixing,
of connecting exposed oxygen to
emulsifying brain sugars—
making juice, if you will—which pushes
back, expanding, blocking
some path and you end

up disappointing the little girl
who reminded you of you
before you were disappointed.
Cold—refreshing in L.A.
a killer in N.Y.—
is a metaphor

for not caring
            for the surface of a bruise
                        for afterward.
                                    It is both adjective and noun,
                                                not needing two words the way
                                                    hot needs heat to become itself.

Cold uses itself to stop change
            one-handed. Water's thicker than blood
                        if it's cold enough outside
                                    and family doesn't know
                                                you don't wear their coat anymore
                                                    you just took your arms and left.

Will you assume we are free
            when we can finally
                        merely pay for ourselves?
                                    Free means both costs nothing
                                                and unbeholden. How can we be free
                                                    when it costs so much to live?

How can one word carry
            both values when the only path
                        to one's own day is to try and steal
                                    it back from those who pay you
                                                to hand it over willingly?
                                                    When what guarantees

us is money? If my daughter learns to be free
            of me will I be glad she has the means
                        to or will I see only my own failure
                                    to be needed, that cell
                                                always waiting to hold me
                                                    carceral, or cancerous?

I believe I love my freedom
                        but is it mine, or stolen?
                           Is it even freedom
                                 if I bought it by buying education
                                        on credit I was "given"
                                                for work not yet secured?

That's some twisted shut
                    mouth of self to future self:
                        no freedom when there's a payment
                                due on the mango-fed cow urine in our art.
                                        The facts keep me company.
                                        I am disgusted, freely.

IV.

If only humor weren't so desperate
      for sweetness.
       If only I could laugh
        in my sleep
         marooned by want
          OK any fucking time.

What if I want you
    eight ways and can only
     have none?
       Would you laugh anyway,
        say you have me now,
         on this page

that is lonely, flat, unbodied
    but not unreal
     for you are shaped here
       an idea of my hands shaping
        themselves around
         your outer outline

and speaking directly to your inner
    lips which are silent
     but responsive
      not to being touched but to being
       written about, written—
        made text of.

Is it true the key to concentration
    is subtraction—eliminate
     all but one object, yes, to focus on?
      But then that object is observed
       in no context, without interrelation
        or shape-giving definition.

A lamp in space is what gives light
        to write this, years ago in light years.
            In space a lamp is part of a cluster
              of bodies flung by gravity
              not a lamp at all—
              it has no one to write under it except us.

Right now, the writer claimed
        that concentration needs subtraction.
            Space is a context
              (maybe the ultimate one?)
                  So the key
                    to concentration

is materially and imaginatively
        impossible,
          the continued reduction
              . . . of what?
                Extra Info?
                   . . . ?

Concentration dissolves and focus fails.
        Laser thought zaps, in its hurry,
          anything lying around.
            Thought takes itself too seriously.
              It's just a soup of blips!
                It's not the world itself.

Thought's all thinking:
      I'm the only one smart enough to figure it all out.
      So now I have to when I'd rather
        use my free time more wisely.
          As in: not do what I have to do
            because no one else can,

but what I'd want to do
                if I didn't have to live
                        up to what everyone always says about me.
                                That I am the only way to solve anything.
                                That I am freedom itself.
                                        That nothing would start

without me.
                I am so busy with all this work,
                        these assignments, these contracts and promises.
                                I never get a moment to be nothing.
                                        To wander without destination,
                                                without accountability,

with my own freedom.
                Exploring my own body and soul
                                on my terms.
                                What would that
                                        be like?
                                                What an idea!

V.

Is there an empirical me ruling
                its population of one
                      through the provinces of memory,
                          physical being, idea production,
                          propulsion
                                through time and space,

and into outlying territories?
                  The totality of a human
                      in its domain,
                        its bodies,
                          ideas, inscription, legacy,
                              what overflows the life?

So the self as a self
                plus self as it affects other nouns
                      and those nouns' verbs.
                          It's such a drag to write this.
                            I always wanted self
                              to be a magic scroll

the universe kept safe,
                taking it out to read
                      longingly sometimes.
                          Then locking it up safe again.
                            Destiny being existence
                              with purpose. That's it.

Nothing so drastic
                as a hero's journey
                      or greatness in perpetuity
                          rather to be held
                            precious by a force
                                of magnanimity

and tenderness,
                    held with love
                              which is timelessness itself.
                                        In this way
                                                  the self lives
                                                            forever.

But not if we're just electric pulses!
                    Activated particles
                              fulfilling the chemical reactions,
                                                  their properties prophesied.
                                                            A done deal.
                                                                      Cooked.

And what is real
                    really is just realistic
                              —my life life-like.
                                        What is "just" is really just
                                                  that minimizer of a word,
                                                            that pointing out

of diminishment. What is true is true
                    enough so long it's eventually
                              more *enough* than truth.
                                        What is actual is actuarial—real ways
                                                  you die by the numbers,
                                                            running

with that wild data set,
                    in the risky section of the table.
                              Hard to argue with the facts,
                                        as they have played
                                                  out historically,
                                                            given the data

it's predicted that you will die
                    by actuary—destined to die
                         by their own glowing hand,
                                   doing the will of the deceased.
                                        Actual actuaries
                                             take the deceased's

numbers and make them fit
                    the living. But it's a bet, a gamble
                         —a risk posing as math, as fact.
                              This is long,
                                   how life is.
                                        You never

know.
Not even after the fact
               no matter how you roll,
                    the dice or down the hill
                              in grassy summer
                                   like you used to.
                                        How long?

VI.

I learned new hell on my own,
                    I copied my own fingerprint
                          in digital pen for an art website
                                    meant to give me free publicity
                                          and a listing in the system
                                                if anything goes wrong.

They can look me up and see my art,
                    and find out if I did it or not.
                          I paint parking lines on the asphalt,
                                    my fault but mislining is not a crime.
                                          Just an accident
                                                waiting to happen.

My thoughts are impeded by fear:
                    I don't want to know
                          what's coming before I have to.
                                    Experience isn't expertise;
                                          isn't egg-sell-ence
                                                (when you've sold

your eggs really well).
                    I congratulate myself and others
                          too easily for what is a congratulant?
                                    One who's been congratulated,
                                          experiences congratsis?
                                                Grateful but boastful?

It is worse than it was.
                    That's when we need support—
                          when it was. When it supposed to be.
                                    What comes next?
                                          is hardly a question
                                                it's a door stopper.

Pretending there's a barrier
           when you can go through
                    any time and will.
                            You can always get at me,
                                    future, if I keep running away
                                            toward you.

Writing is not a sensory art,
                it's barely of the material world,
                          two dimensions only.
                                  The paper isn't the writing.
                                      Its thickness is
                                          a mere mounting, a mat.

Words, even written, have to jump
                and attach themselves
                          like three monkeys to sensation,
                                  to thingness. We think we see words,
                                      hear them, because we are
                                          animals with instincts

to guide us to what is real and ionic—not i ron⎮ ic⎮—
                and words don't land on the "food and scat"
                        side of the divide.
                              Words fall through the air
                                  maybe caught by a sheet
                                        like someone jumped

out the third story window
                of a burning house,
                        also a sheet stretched out below
                              by some writer
                                  who also read the rain and so has
                                      sniffed out the need for the sheet.

To lend substance to the unbodied words
              who do not bounce
                   and are not saved.
                            Writing is a verb ("I'm ___,")
                            and noun ("my ___,")
                               and an adjective ("___ time/life.")

Is there a whole jar full of words like that?
              Any word could slip into a new category
                   nothing material to block it—
                        only ideology, which is why
                            I can't tell you what I wrote
                               without rewriting it, in speech.

Which is why I can't speak at all
              without nouning my verbs
                   and adjectivizing my nouns
                      like an animal who smells fire
                         and runs before the smoke begins
                               to curl and crawl in earnest.

VII.

If you scratch the surface of writing
$\qquad$ you chip the letters right off
$\qquad$ the page which erases them.
$\qquad$ You can't go deeper materially.
$\qquad$ To absorb words, you must lower
$\qquad$ a sensory organ into it and let it stew and

steep until the meaning is leached
$\qquad$ from the page and dispersed
$\qquad$ through your eyes,
$\qquad$ pouring a meaning-tea into your brain
$\qquad$ or some unknown part of your brain—
$\qquad$ is language spoken only in one area?

Why doesn't language know the ways
$\qquad$ other parts of the brain communicate?
$\qquad$ Why does language stop at itself,
$\qquad$ stubborn tourist. Poetry is allowed
$\qquad$ to follow the self-in-thoughts
$\qquad$ on its way to the body it lives in

and the bodies and minds of those
$\qquad$ who might read it. This opening,
$\qquad$ this lit path, gives the impression
$\qquad$ poetry is trusted, and will be
$\qquad$ given access but each threshold
$\qquad$ and gate (each bower and gazebo,

each bedside and website)
$\qquad$ has a new password poetry may not know.
$\qquad$ Poetry may have forgotten.
$\qquad$ The body is an anemone,
$\qquad$ creature who knows when to hold them,
$\qquad$ knows when to fold them,

and does not gamble like a gambler
                    who learns "hit me" literally
                    and is open to losing his home,
                                his aim, last dime, last name.
                                    The body does not
                                            just let any poetry in,

mostly just lets it play
                    in the yard of the head,
                    like a squirrel.
                        What if the Wheel of Fortune
                                was a hand-less clock
                                    and there was no marking

or measurement of tempo
                    no documentation on the face of it
                        just spinning freely, downhill,
                        arms pinwheeling
                                like the button wheel pinned to a TP tube car
                                            made by a child.

Pipe cleaner axles.
                    The thing everyone says about the Wheel
                        of Fortune is that you must
                            somehow climb to the center,
                                sit right on the pin so you don't get crushed
                                        when the wheel edge is down.

So you don't drink
                    all the champagne when it's up.
                        And yet Time's arms stretch
                                out to the clock's edge,
                                    minute hand reaching hard,
                                        the hour hand, more tentative,

thinking: *do I really want to change?*
           We call it stress but what is it really?
                      Pressure, emphasis, a squeeze
                                 being held securely
                                            by potential disaster
                                                       until it becomes actual?

A tightening, a well feeling with ill water,
                      a crackling crystal dragging through.
                                 veins, slicing them open
                                            from the inside, hairline of blood
                                                       thickening behind the edge
                                                                  cutting as it goes—

you know it's there you feel it
                      like you feel a flash before you see it,
                                 the pain, just before it comes.
                                            And yet there is no pain. Only pressure.
                                                       Sick weight holding down the bone
                                                                  compressing the meat,

breaking down the fibers,
                      popping the muscle
                                 into mush, crushed.
                                            The power of stress
                                                       is mind over matter.
                                                                  I don't mind. It doesn't matter.

VIII.

To fill a page to open a mind,

        lift a hand, write a line,

          and keep that line alive

               through years of words: your body

                  must be your own no question

                     no hesitation given. Your body,

to you from you.

        Your mind, too, changeable

          irreversible touchable, ready to accept

               another into itself,

                  changing the mind inside out.

                     With mind, it's all inside,

nothing out, no divide,

        no part without the other

          no fire without before fire and after fire.

               You can make your voice

                  sound younger or softer ·

                     more open to interpretation

but mostly yes, sexier than you are.

        It's basic that people react strongly

          to the sound of your voice.

               It practically is you and we know it.

                  Not talking is selfish. Not listening is

                     aggressive, blocking,

a person saying no you will not have a say,

        will not be heard is saying:

          you aren't you with me.

               I don't need a story or a song

                  but people did so they invented

                     tunes and tales—cute, right?

OK I do need a song and story,
        they can be the same.
              If mine, they will be.
                    The song is notably round sounding
                  and the story all flat angles
                      not very promising but I work on it.

I like to choose beautiful sounds but I often can't,
          I need to be told something
              besides *isn't it beautiful*
                  for a while listening to this.
                    I don't believe you saying that can't be
                      your story. It ends. It hardly begins

and has already spoken for (me).
        If the words don't try
           to be what they're not,
              only say what is, will they be obvious
                and/or genuine?
                    If the words don't mean

what they think they mean
        who is talking?
        What do words think
              they mean if not their own ideal?
                  The corresponding
                    and perfect thing

to match or complete or make real the usability
          and fit of a word
             with meaning: of love
              to love's lover. I'll say nothing
                if I think you think
                  what I'll say is nothing.

I'll talk all night in your voice
        if I think it makes you listen.
                Does everyone feel unheard?
                Or just writers?
                    Do others have a blue-black
                        lump in throat,

so afraid to speak, or only poets?
        Do poets only ever really speak
            to other poets or are there other poets
                for other poets to talk to?
                    Nobody can hear me, I stutter

and mumble. Not secretly
        hostile or self-sabotaging,
            but because I wanted to be heard
                too badly and I crashed my soul
                  into my meaning
                    and flub and flap too fast

and can't hear
        and I'm so impatient, ever alone.
            Nobody gives chances—we trade in trust.
                We choose to trust someone but
                  there's no chance
                    you're not being used

by someone who benefits from your trust
        and the way you can trick yourself.
            Being used isn't talked about
                as much as it happens.
                  Not just sex but books
                    are sex so books too, the folks

who buy and sell books.
Who read and recommend,
use and lose, burn or give away,
ignore, forget, rave, quote.
Yes sure, they think your book
is good. They tell you that,

and other things
about yourself and don't tell you
some things too.
Things you might want to know.
Maybe they care about you
aside from the books. I hope so.

But you, your book is you.
To them, your book is you, but theirs.
You see? They love the you
that is theirs (your book).
And so they
position you

for special experiences,
where you have a mic or are in Biz Class
or a room full of people
with your book on their lap and flowers.
Checks with which you say
I will buy

flowers too. And these nice temporary things
are your payment for giving
your publisher what you
wrote and they wanted
and bought and which you sold to them.
You see? It's not your body.

Not your mind. Products
                    of your body and mind,
                         a thing with no life of its own,
                              filled with your lived life still twitching.
                                   And it's not dead, not dying.
                                        But it must be said,

a kind of paper zombie,
          original flat origami zombie
                    but with no folds only markings (yours),
                         cut edges, corners, glued together
                              cardboard boxish
                                   thin brickish

dust and shreds bound by thread
               sometimes, sewn down
                    where edge meets selvedge.
                         It doesn't know it exists.
                              Why did they take/make my book?
                                   Didn't they know it was me

they bound? Me they described
               as un-putdownable and deft?
                    Not knowing in advance
                         is the piece that changes
                              everything about the future.
                                   Is the world real

or am I clinging to some un-world
               I think exists in its place?
                    If you only knew one alphabet
                         how do you know
                              Russian reverses N
                                   and Japanese reads from right to left

and tell me here in English
                    it's our direction that always seems cursed
                              by its opposite. Still the river flows.
                                        Land can't be fully assimilated
                                                  under the rules of math, or language—
                                                            land may be bought or sold but

it cannot be said to be ruled.
              And Time has its own rules,
                        though not speaking
                                  the same language,
                                            Time doesn't call them rules
                                                      and since I know Time's language
                                                                just a little

(enough to get by on in a restaurant
                    for example) I know it doesn't
                              think it goes by rules,
                                        that it's not going in a circle, for example,
                                                  knows it goes around but in

a spiral, either up or down.
              That's not part of Time's lexicon
                        or body—up or down, or neither.
                                  Time thinks it goes the way it goes,
                                            any old way, nothing grinding on it but
                                                      nothing guiding its path, no way
                                                                of knowing that one may be right.

To have the wrong time.
              A good Time, but the wrong one.
                        Don't know that's something people
                                  living outside Time's mind consider
                                            important, even a guiding principle.
                                                      The idea of principle,

the existence of ideas, isn't relevant
           to Time that's why we chase it
               demand it mean something
                    accused of everything
                         we don't get
                            to do or be.

But land understands Time's mind,
           they know it's not measured in minutes or yards
               but who is around and who to share
                    everything with.
                      And that every last real
                         experience might be blotted out,

vanished, perished. Punished,
           by no mind that knows anything of you,
               but now is you.

IX.

Your need is yours, I'm not grateful.

You need to give me

what is not a gift, to me,

but a feeling of lessened need, for you.

When you say you do you mean me?

When I say you I mean me.

I mean how are we not both what I always mean?

I am you, worn inside out alone

in a hall of mirrors with no edges,

or dimension other than depth,

having fallen all the way in

so there's no ripple, no crack,

no back to us for us.

Sometimes all that matters

is being able to finish a thought,

whereas before, the problem was others

interrupting me, but now

I just lose my way.

I don't want to live so long someone has to

increasingly take care of me, so increasingly

that it has to be an employee

or is that too terrible to say?

I don't want it for me

but for others OK?

What is an independent life? What defines it—

why is it so important? Why do we fight for it

but everything's weighted against it

eventually, for each of us, really

in the end. Will we die independent?

Any of us not somebody's job? Somebody whose job it is to keep me
    plugged into a generator
      if the power goes out?
        That's not a metaphor. Or it is, for life.
         That is death is a metaphor for life,
          death is like life but less believable.

I don't think I'm brainy because I love too much
    the feeling of my thoughts moving
      aside to let new ones in,
       and the mixing feels so good,
        I begin to crave it, look for it,
         hard books, out-there arguments,

paintings, phrases I turn over
    for meaning underneath
     and accept the hole is in me.
      The absence, thick suction,
       where better ideas will sink into mine
       like a lush bed of all the flowers

whose names I could learn. I am jealous of myself
    writing here ~~as I'm dying~~ as I'm doing now.
    I know when I come here again
      I will be reading this, not writing it,
      wishing I were. Writing isn't pleasant,
       not relaxing, doesn't feel exciting,

the tip of a pen is the line of life lived
    truthfully and fully and that line
    both led and followed that life.
      But writing is not illuminating like that,
       not profound. Usually it's ink motion,
        a liquid to remind you of flow.

Where there is flow, what you know finds form.
                    Draws near to the surface so your pen
                              can trace the features, expressions.
                                        Flow is sound-blocking, interruption
                                        can't rise to it, face set
                                                  to the clock of work.

Try to turn my mind away from the lines
                    and shapes of meaning and the best
                         you get is a hollow corner
                              snapped off the edge, a crumpled slip
                                   of my attention. The whole won't be
                                        available for anything else

but this ink, while it flows inside my pen
                    moved by that energy I must call flow.
                         Another word for it is overflow,
                              brimming? An explosion?
                                   Water living life post-vessel?
                                        But nothing is wasted, nothing runs.

X.

"Ruin" is "I run"

with the *I* jumping ahead

to outrun the ruin.

Happens with "fluid" and "I flud"

too but here the *I* causes the flud

by jumping ship, absence miring it

as well as a misspelling

which I'm on the fence about.

Some people don't know

where their *I* falls whatever word they're in.

There is no I in fall.

No I in grammar or syntax,

only spelling. But I don't make the rules.

Some good ideas are called bad ideas,

and immediately we disbelieve in them.

Like fast writing or calling it mind-wind.

Or living with someone.

Are you in a room? Is it roomy?

Or are you still making do in small spaces,

afraid of outside ones, what's there?

Having a roommate is

like having a wilderness all to yourself.

She was magical like all girls—

have you ever met an ordinary one?

I never met a Tanya with metal as a signature

scent called Lock Sex and was a string

of beads that were actually eyes.

You know I've been wanting to write

about you for over thirty years.

You knew I eventually would.

You probably guessed I'd hide you here,
                    in a long, careening poem, making you
                              as hard to find as you are.
                                        I waited until you were really gone
                                                  but I think you are not dead,
                                                            just gone to me. And maybe if you read

this you'll find me again.
                    If you want to, that is, I'm easy.
                              Even if you don't think so.
                                        Were you last in Malaysia? Spain? Why?
                                                  You always knew this fathered
                                                            world wouldn't let you

do shit.

And the shit you wanted to do was love art sex
                    and more love and more art, in that order.
                              What did I do to make you leave me
                                        as if you hated me? I must have been fatherly.
                                                  The only thing anyone could do
                                                            that you found unforgivable.

It seemed like you slept with everybody but really
                    they slept with you and you were trying
                              people out and on.
                                        You wanted to know who there was to love.
                                                  What there was to it. Was great love,
                                                            like great art, possible, and did it need to

go through great sex to get to it?
                    Could there be a way to or way out
                              of love that was not through use?
                                        That just was,
                                                  just to be a way in itself,
                                                            like art could be?

Art—useless but for providing proof that uselessness
                     was good because [transitive property]
                          art was good and art could
                                        be useful and useless at the same time,
                                     and that its value
                                            doesn't hang on that balance

—but then money came into it and ruined everything
                     Tanya tried to build around her holy Trinity,
                              which was by far the best holy Trinity.
                                   Those questions she threw
                                       herself so completely into
                                           were mine too but I was afraid.

I thought I had something to lose,
                some womanhood or pride.
                          If I were more brave
                                less afraid of losing love
                                        —no, afraid of not being liked—
                                             I'd have stood with you.

I was afraid of making mistakes.
          But I couldn't learn from yours, of course,
                          no matter what I thought.
                              I thought it was possible to "ruin"
                                        one's life. I was afraid of you
                                             because you didn't agree.

I wasn't you, wasn't like you
          wouldn't bounce like you:
                    I'd be hurt. I didn't see
                              you were hurt too.
                                   And you didn't hide it—I looked away.
                                        What IS that in me?

I've done it since then
        repeatedly, when my worst fear
                is coming, soon, to be.
                        I could have predicted you'd flee.
                            Oh that attitude: ("I know you")
                                we both hated in each other.

You were proprietary, thought you knew me,
            felt threatened when I changed.
                    When I fell in love with Camilla,
                            you fled before meeting her.
                                In my city for one night,
                                    stood us up at the restaurant.

Something natural
        in the city wind singing
                    to the rhythm run ahead:
                            where you're going will you
                                take me will you take me with you
                                            if you go?

I never saw you again,
            you called me to say I was the worst—
                    I guess not something you could say
                            at dinner with my new love.
                                You felt silenced. Fell silent.
                                    I didn't break it.

XI.

That taught me to read other friends later: if they bailed
moments before meeting my partner it meant
they were secretly in love with me
and that is true. It happened two times.
You wanted to be wanted
so wanting me was a way

to show me how you wanted to be treated by me.
But I failed or was stubborn or needed
someone to push against.
Or I was being eaten alive.
These resentments grow until you
can no longer bear the sight

of the person. It happened twice, Tanya.
It happens right before break ups,
where just the energy
coming off the wounded friend/lover
sets you off. That desperate energy
oh I've felt it/done it too,

it's a core of molten guilt, slick oppression,
being silenced and agreeing to it,
knowing I'm right.
And being right always matters.
It was always the person
who was wrong who said

"it doesn't matter who's right." Am I right?
I know I am. It's insufferable.
Who wouldn't leave me
and never come back
if I'm always right this time.
Tanya was my equal

in stubbornness, and artistic zeal
                    but she didn't want me to grow.
                            Why? Did I want her to?
                                    Maybe if she grew away from me
                                        I would have clung.
                                                Instead I found new friends.

Old lovers returning always hear about you.
                    They poke around till they get the dirt:
                            I heard you started smoking
                                    shit like that   *heard you like girls now*
                                        like they think they know
                                                what's best for you and they do.

The secret strength of weakness
                    is that it makes others weak.
                            From there it's easy
                                    for original weakness to recognize
                                        its own child and nourish it,
                                                educate it in the ways

of weakness, to seep.
                    Then weakness grows in numbers
                            in which can be found strength,
                                    and the strength is not secret—
                                        it's also no longer weakness
                                                but power and always was.

"Power over" isn't from a different dimension than "power under,"
                    the powered-under are merely ruled or governed
                            not squashed. And if you've been
                                    governed and survive you feel fine
                                        about other people suffering—
                                                or not fine, rather proud.

Like you made it by being weak in an acceptable way all along.
I need to be scarce but want to be surrounded
by heavy known objects, how strange
is solidity how scary a farce is safety.
Even the word sounds sarcastic all by itself.
Safety.

A "safety" belt for those occasions
when a semi crushes your Honda Fit.
The word itself knows
it could never be true.
It can only ever be a slippery floor
of a concept. Taking a safe

not to crack it but to try to tip it as if, if you do this,
it won't fall out the window of a high-rise
right onto you as you walk under it.
But you blew it—not being a cartoon
turned it tragic, always the answer
to the question of safety.

XII.

Locked in, every key sets two free

                but safety is an inmate. I bought a fireproof,

                    waterproof, zippered file,

                          to keep my manuscripts safe while I worked

                              on them. I became conscious of fire

                                  and flood whenever I wrote.

I imagined some great treasure

                lost by a spark, the same spark I'd used

                    to write by, pleased to have saved

                        my work. Perhaps the flood

                            was the real danger:

                              put your safe in the dishwasher

to keep it safe from fire but the dishwasher

                gets pushed on and the inside floods

                    and rusts your good safe shut for good.

                        The fountain pen I kept in the folder

                            exploded and splotched

                              and soaked every page.

All the ink I didn't write with blotted out all I did.

                But my zipper file remained, no ink stained

                    my desk or bed. My work,

                      all the work of many nights,

                          lost before I could load it

                            into a cloud, for free.

Things are falling down, stars overhead,

                all around the stairs, through the wars

                    and the fears, through the years,

                        started falling, startling no one,

                          long before you—

                            looked up,

looked around
        they fell flat and hard and far,
            we can't see what the things are
                or where they fell from
                    whether we were well then and there
                        and not now or here,

or were just about to fall, apart,
        fall hard and fast, the way it did last time
            or if this time it would last.
                Parents of grown children tell me grown children
                    leave but you can't touch their rooms.
                        And you can't leave.

You have to stay there for when they come back,
        like you're a paused video but they forget
            to watch you when they come back.
                Or they don't come back
                    so you're like the mom in *The Leftovers*
                      doing chores for nobody.

At least the dog appreciates you, at least she needs you
        for your general needs-meeting skills.
            Don't you have a dog
                to play with somewhere, my child?
                    Can't you get completely engrossed
                      in a project all day?

What about the science kits—those make-your-own fertilizer
        hair clips with rhinestones and chemical reactions
            of slime and purple smoke?
                Can you leave me alone now, and promise
                  to come sit by your old mom
                      when I am old

and you are able to run off and find your own chemistry
                projects and watch your own smoke dissipate,
                        never colorful again,
                        in a cold apartment in the city without me.
                                The kids, they say, become you,
                                        but they live, so that's a happy story.

They live elsewhere—they were able to move,
                they found their own place.
                        Sounds like they're real
                                independent, self-sufficient, responsible,
                                        rich off your money, ungrateful,
                                                naturally averse to you anymore.

We used to live in the city that kept us
                in grand digs and underwater,
                        like Urashima Taro,
                                the boy who visited the old sea turtle's Royal Palace.
                                The boy went for a long weekend, returned
                                        home 200 years later, everyone dead.

Will you return that way?
                (The way is both
                a way and a question:
                                        will you go the way going goes
                                                or will you go the way
                                                        the way goes?)

Ancient, unaware, so sure
                we spent time in the same denominations
                        as everyone else, but we had to
                                turn back to the palace, un-Kings we,
                                        duchesses of dust,
                                                for the city can't die without us.

We used to dream of a little place in the city,
a *pied-à-terre,* but that's the worst idea:
to want so badly to live
in the city you get a place to NOT live in, there.
Really, you live elsewhere
where you never wanted to live

but do, like wet cut flowers, spilling.
I can't write an ending for posterity.
Too much future all sung out—
old love, no longer "dead to me"
you are completely mixed up
with the rest of me, ever.

Do I refract everything I experience
through everyone I experience—
inhaling 1991 Tanya,
exhaling present self?
I know I'll never know.
But I'm writing this toward that

knowledge of endless unknowing.
That is why writers are so weird,
that and other reasons,
we are neither creative nor interpretive artists but both.
And those two lives are hard to live
at once, believe me, I'm trying.

ACKNOWLEDGMENTS

This is a book about mentorship. I can't thank mine nearly enough, but I can name them here: Wendy Brown, Helene Moglen, Bettina Aptheker, Donna Haraway, Marcine Solarez, Lucie Brock-Broido, Richard Howard, Lucille Clifton, Mark Doty, Marilyn Hacker, Susan Sontag, and Dorothea Tanning.

Thank you to Deborah Garrison, for her singular brilliance, great eye, and full-hearted guidance: what joy it is to be edited by you, to be understood by you. Thank you to Zuleima Ugalde and everyone at Knopf, a dream publisher.

Gratitude for my inspiring work family at Rutgers University—Newark: Rigoberto González, Alice Elliott Dark, Naomi Jackson, Akil Kumarasamy, John Keene, James Goodman, Rachel Hadas, Cathy Park Hong, and our extraordinary dean of arts and sciences, Jacqueline Mattis. My marvelous colleagues teach me, daily, the good work of mentoring in a creative/learning community. Thank you to my wonderful students.

This book exists in large part because I was granted space and time by MacDowell, during the pandemic, in December 2020. Thank you, MacDowell.

More love and thanks to friends of my soul who guided this book with their example, art, companionship, critical eye, or support/care: Hilton Als, Robin Coste Lewis, Paola Prestini, Jessica Rankin, Jennie C. Jones, Natalie Diaz, Deborah Landau, Mark Bibbins, Jennifer Grotz, Franklin Sirmans, Kevin Young, Natasha Trethewey, Tina Chang, Dana Jaye Cadman, Kate Clinton, Amy Herzog, Rachel Eliza Griffiths, Mark Wunderlich, and my eternal flames, the Pretendettes.

Thank you to Lisa, my sister. Thank you to Tanya, my first roommate at University of California, Santa Cruz, wherever you are now.

To mark the moment, the year, the era, I want to say good-bye here to people I still love: Ellis Avery, Kamilah Aisha Moon, Urvashi Vaid, and my one and only dad, Robert P. Shaughnessy.

I am grateful for the incredible women who keep my family whole: Wendy

Gould-Nogueira and Diana Brown. And for my family: Cal and Simone, you have and are my heart. Craig, you carry my heart in your heart and I know it is safe. I love you.

. . .

"Tell Our Mothers We Tell Ourselves the Story . . ." was commissioned by the National Museum of Norway for the opening of the National Museum of Art, Architecture and Design in Oslo for the 2022–2023 exhibition catalog for Laure Prouvost's installation, editor Marianne Yvenes.

"The Impossible Lesbian Love Object(s)" was commissioned by the Museum of Modern Art for their magazine's Poetry Project, 2019, curator/editor Leah Dickerman, editor Robin Coste Lewis.

"On *The Shaded Line* by Lauren Lovette" was commissioned by the New York City Ballet for their Poems of Gesture series, 2020, editor Michaela Drapes.

"Who Sings Whose Songs?," "On *Loss of Feathers* by Ursula von Rydingsvard," and "On *Romeu, 'My Deer'* by Berlinde De Bruyckere" were commissioned by the Drawing Center's exhibition and book *Ways of Seeing: Writings on Drawings from the Jack Shear Collection,* 2021, editors Claire Gilman and Hilton Als.

"For the Matter to Mean and the Meaning Matter" was commissioned for the catalog of Toba Khedoori's solo exhibition at the Los Angeles County Museum of Art, 2016–2017, *Toba Khedoori,* publisher Lisa Mark, editor Claire Crighton.

"The Poets Are Dying" appeared in *The New Yorker,* October 28, 2019.

"Coursework" was delivered as a virtual reading at Writing for Living: A Conference in Honor of Helene Moglen, University of California, Santa Cruz, 2021.

"Moving Far Away," "Tell Our Mothers We Tell Ourselves the Story . . . ," "The Impossible Lesbian Love Object(s)," "The Artist Jessica Rankin," "What Have I Done?," "On *Loss of Feathers* . . . ," and "Who Sings Whose Songs?" appeared in *Liquid Flesh: New & Selected Poems* by Bloodaxe Books in Fall 2022, editor Neil Astley.

A NOTE ABOUT THE AUTHOR

Brenda Shaughnessy is the Okinawan-Irish American author of five previous books of poetry, including *The Octopus Museum* and *Our Andromeda*. The recipient of a 2018 Literature Award from the American Academy of Arts and Letters, and a professor of English and creative writing at Rutgers University—Newark, Shaughnessy lives with her family in New Jersey.

A NOTE ON THE TYPE

The text of this book was set in Filosofia, a typeface designed by Zuzana Licko in 1996 as a revival of the typefaces of Giambattista Bodoni (1740–1813).

Licko, born in Bratislava, Czechoslovakia, in 1961, is the cofounder of Emigre, a digital type foundry. Emigre was one of the first independent type foundries to establish itself centered around personal computer technology.

Composed by North Market Street Graphics, Lancaster, Pennsylvania

Printed and bound by Lakeside Book Company, Harrisonburg, Virginia

Designed by Maggie Hinders